Chinese Cut-Paper Designs

Selected by Theodore Menten

Dover Publications, Inc., New York

Publisher's Note

The art of cutting paper into designs is attested in China (where paper was invented) as early as the Tang Dynasty (618-906). It may have originated as a courtly pastime, but it is best known from more recent times as a folk art practiced in all parts of the country.

These cutouts are pasted onto walls, windows and other parts of houses and onto numerous smaller objects, where they serve not only as ornaments but also as good-luck charms. Some are also used as embroidery patterns. At festival times particularly, cut-paper designs are sold in the streets, given as greetings or gifts and proudly displayed by the recipients.

Many are prepared wholly by skillful manipulation of scissors, but others (especially those done by professional or semiprofessional makers) involve the use of knives, gouges, punches and even needles. Sometimes dozens of sheets are secured in a wooden frame and cut through at once. The paper is dyed in a variety of (generally solid) colors.

Like many other peasant arts, cut-paper designs are now being encouraged by the Chinese authorities. The present volume, entirely reproduced from originals, offers a wide selection of modern designs, some traditional in style, some more Western-looking.

Among the subjects represented are real and mythical animals and birds (panda, phoenix, dragon, tiger, crane, etc.), flowers and fruits, fish, insects, lanterns, children performing everyday activities, scenes and characters from fiction (especially the Monkey King), the Great Wall, ancient bronze ceremonial vessels, and numerous others.

Published in Canada by General Publishing Company, Ltd., 30 Lesmill Road, Don Mills, Toronto, Ontario.

Published in the United Kingdom by Constable and Company, Ltd., 10 Orange Street, London WC 2.

Chinese Cut-Paper Designs is a new work, first published by Dover Publications, Inc., in 1975.

International Standard Book Number: 0-486-23198-4
Library of Congress Catalog Card Number: 75-22240

Manufactured in the United States of America
Dover Publications, Inc.
180 Varick Street
New York, N.Y. 10014

17

43

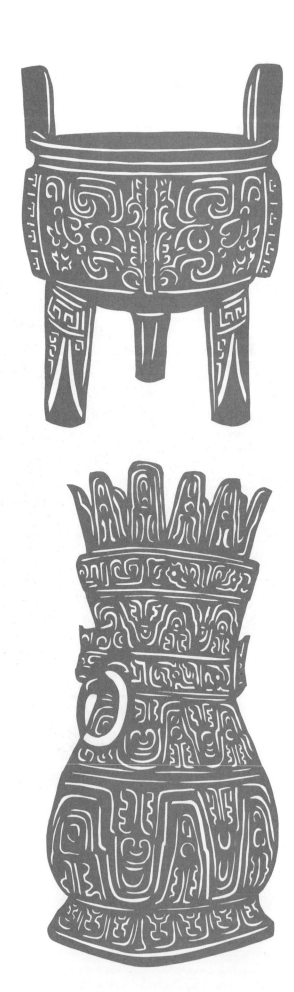